Cultural Insanity

And the roadmap to
GREAT ORGANISATIONAL CULTURE

ROSS JUDD

First published in 2019 by Ross Judd

All inquiries should be made to the author.
team@teamfocus.com.au
www.teamfocus.com.au

A catalogue entry for this book is available from the National Library of Australia.

ISBN: 978-1-925921-43-4

Project management and text design by Michael Hanrahan Publishing
Cover design by Peter Reardon
Illustrations by Jock Macneish (www.strategicimages.com.au)

Disclaimer

Contents

Contents

Introduction
The power of culture

Institutional culture has been making the headlines in recent years. It has been raised in scandals involving international business, sport, non-profit organisations and even religion. The reports into scandals such as Volkswagen 'Dieselgate', the collapse of Lehman Brothers, the Royal Commission into Banking in Australia, and the 'ball tampering' scandal in Australian cricket have all talked about how a 'culture was allowed to develop' that tolerated, supported, and even encouraged the decisions of the individuals involved.

It's worth noting that organisational culture is being cited as a contributing factor in illegal and scandalous activity. And the reports often take it one step further and suggest that culture can drive an individual to make decisions and take actions *contrary to their own values and beliefs*. It's a strong statement about the influence of culture, and the responsibility of leaders to create the *right* culture.

What other part of organisational life has that much power?

Leaders must take note. And they must know how to respond.

The driving force in any organisation

Imagine this. You walk into a store. You walk past staff who are engaged in a deep personal conversation. At the back of the store you find product on the floor and shelves in a mess. It's one of a chain of stores that has a reputation for being well managed. The staff have received training, instruction from their manager, and other incentives to keep the store tidy. And yet, it's a mess.

Why?

The training and systems are in place. People have the resources they need.

So, *why does this happen?*

It's because a culture has been allowed to develop that tolerates, supports, and even encourages the decisions of these individuals. In this simple example they have decided to ignore their responsibilities and 'have a chat'. They are being influenced by the culture.

Culture is the driving force in any organisation, including yours. It has more influence than you, your leadership team, systems, training programs, or anything else.

If the culture throughout the business is simply to 'let things go' then that's what will happen. A strong leader will correct such behaviour, but if that leader is not around, people will revert to the cultural expectations of the people around them. A strong company will create systems to try to drive the right behaviour, but systems won't solve these issues if they are not supported by the culture.

A scary thought

To get the best out of your organisation and achieve great outcomes, you need to create a culture where people expect and demand the right behaviour *from each other*.

You need to create a strong *cultural expectation*.

For most leaders that's a scary thought, mainly because culture is something they don't understand, can't define, and have no idea how to 'create' or 'change' – even though it's often a topic of conversation.

To make matters worse, the industry, consultants and products that have sprung up to help *aren't* actually helping. They are confusing and complicating the issue. They're asking leaders to navigate complex surveys, remember unwieldy definitions and terms, implement complicated processes, and meet unrealistic expectations.

It's cultural insanity.

Developing a strong culture should be a simple and natural process that connects and engages people in healthy and profitable discussions, but instead it has become a poison chalice full of complications that most leaders have no idea how to 'manage'. It's made even harder if you talk about 'culture change' because that will make people defensive. They will hear the message as either, 'your culture is bad and needs to change', or, 'we're implementing another change program'.

Add to that complex surveys, apps that monitor behaviour, and processes people struggle to understand, and you will have suspicious and cynical people.

Sound familiar?

Trying to 'change' culture, or using a 'change management approach' to culture, is like trying to push a big blob of jelly up a hill. The bit you are pushing on will appear to move but other parts of the blob will fold back around you, and if you get lopsided it will all slide out of your control and blob its way back down the hill.

Can't we just try harder?

When it's not working, most people just push harder on the blob. That's like speaking more slowly or yelling more loudly when someone who speaks another language doesn't understand you.

Instead of simplifying the process and making it something that's easy to achieve and that creates a fantastic bond between a leader and their team, we're making it more complicated, and people are becoming more disillusioned. In the words of Albert Einstein, people are doing the same thing over and over again and expecting a different result.

Which is insane.

Good culture is something everyone wants

You should be having the opposite experience in your organisation.

A good culture is something everyone wants, so creating it should be natural, simple, and engaging. Even your most jaded, cynical, negative employee wants to be part of a great culture.

If you need to be convinced, think about what happens if you talk about improving the culture in your business and don't follow through. If you've never had that experience, just imagine how people would react. You'll end up in a worse situation because people initially get excited, and then become angry and disillusioned when they are let down.

Early in my career I had the opportunity to work with a small engineering division in a large company. They employed 300 people and created signalling solutions for railway crossings.

The GM realised the culture was poor and was causing people to leave. He had lost 50 people in one year and was struggling to recruit good-quality engineers. They were even going to the expense of advertising and bringing candidates in from overseas. He knew he needed help.

He wanted to start with a review of the culture. I advised him to make sure he had the full backing of his Executive General Manager for the budget that would follow. There was no doubt a development program would be needed once the assessment was finished, and I knew what would happen if we didn't follow through.

I was assured we had the full backing of his EGM.

We did the assessment, went around Australia letting people know what we had uncovered, built a development plan with input from each area of the business, and presented that plan to the EGM.

It was rejected.

So, we strengthened the financial analysis and demonstrated the significant return on investment that would be achieved.

It was rejected again.

The EGM disagreed with our estimate that addressing the culture and stemming the flow of people leaving the business would save him *millions*.

The next year they lost roughly 100 employees. The following year they were unable to deliver projects, and the division was shut down.

People left because, despite the problems, they had become excited about improving the culture, and then became angry when they were told it wasn't going to happen.

The challenge is belief

Everyone wants to be part of a great culture, but the challenge is they don't *believe* it can happen; in fact, they believe it *won't* happen. They will say things like 'we've heard all this before and nothing changed'.

It doesn't mean they don't want to be part of a great culture; it means they don't believe their leaders are genuine, committed, and humble enough to engage them and create a great culture. Their cynicism is confirmed when their leaders start throwing complex surveys, complicated definitions and 'culture change' programs at them.

How to convince people

The way to convince people that this is not simply a box-ticking exercise and that you are *genuine* about culture, *committed* to greatness, and *humble* enough to listen to their feedback is by *engaging them in the process.*

The simple act of starting a conversation and listening to them will help them *believe* things are different. They will then contribute to the process in a way that will take you well past any benchmark you set for yourself.

The cure

The popular 'culture change' process is back to front.

'Culture change' is based on the idea the person implementing the change is the expert. But you need a process that acknowledges *your people* as the experts. If you let them, *they* will create a great culture. You just need to give them the right information and the opportunity, and get out of the way.

You don't need to run culture change programs *for your people* – you need to engage with them and let them run culture change programs *for you*.

You will achieve much more if you engage with your people and *facilitate* conversations to create the ideal culture.

EGNAHC ERUTLUC !

WHEN DO YOU THINK HE WILL REALISE HE'S GOT IT
THE WRONG WAY ROUND ?

Challenging the usual thinking

As you will see from the definition of culture, creating a healthy culture is as simple as having the right conversations.

Creating a *great* culture needs a specific sequence of conversations, which I've called 'A.D.A.P.T.' It's a handy acronym to help you remember the five simple steps that can lead to an amazing culture, which are explained in this book.

It's not a 'culture change' program; it's simply a 'culture program'. It's a series of conversations that engages your people to create a great culture.

It follows sound principles and is based on the idea that a great culture is purposeful. You are not imposing language, definitions, complex assessments or any of the other challenges associated with 'culture change'. You are talking about the purpose of your organisation and the culture needed to deliver that purpose, and planning a program to bridge the gap from your current to your target culture.

Simple.

How to A.D.A.P.T.

The first step in the A.D.A.P.T. process is to *Align with purpose.* You must align people with why your company, department, division, site, or team exists.

You then engage with your people to *Define* the culture needed to deliver that purpose (that's step 2). You then *Assess* your current culture (step 3), *Plan* (step 4) and *Transform* (step 5).

Best of all, you or somebody in your organisation can be the facilitator for most of the process. The only step that *requires* an external perspective is *assessing current culture* (step 3). Engaging an external facilitator for the other steps in the A.D.A.P.T. process is optional. You would benefit from an external perspective but it's not *essential.*

The *essential* part is that you *have the conversations.*

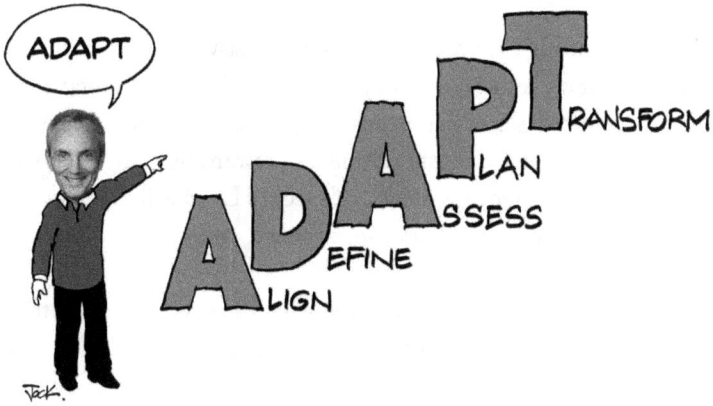

Don't just take my word for it ...

I encourage you to question everything in this book and compare it to your experience. Keep asking yourself 'is that right?' and 'does it make sense?' If it doesn't make sense then you haven't lost much – a bit of time and the price of this book.

If it *does* make sense (which it does), you stand to make enormous gains because you will develop a new understanding of organisational culture and you will have a simple process designed to create a whole new experience.

Everything you need is in the following chapters. It's all here.

There is a practical and useful definition of culture that will help explain what we are talking about and what you need to do as a leader. We then explore the underlying principles and philosophies that should apply to any culture program.

There is also a detailed explanation of each step in the A.D.A.P.T. process. Everything you need to know to implement the process yourself is in these pages.

A great experience

Creating a strong culture should be simple, easy, and a great experience. It's not rocket science, and you don't need a degree in statistics. It's just common sense that needs to become common practice.

It's also one of the most exciting and rewarding things you will ever do. You will enjoy new levels of success. Lives will dramatically improve as people communicate, connect, and create something amazing.

This will give you everything you need to create a *great* culture, and a great culture will give you everything you need to create *greatness*.

Chapter 1

Defining and understanding organisational culture

To understand culture and the huge influence it has on people, think about what you do when you are in a new or unfamiliar situation.

You watch other people, and adjust your behaviour to fit in with their behaviour and *their expectations*.

You've been doing it all your life. When you were young, you watched the adults and role modelled their behaviour. Your behaviour was modified and you learned to adjust to the expectations of your parents, family, and friends.

As you grew up you watched the other students and adopted behaviour based on their expectations. It's now an unconscious habit that is so natural and instinctive you are not even aware it's happening.

It's a trait we all share. We do this because we want and need to be accepted as part of the group. Acceptance is critical to our health and wellbeing. We want to avoid doing something stupid or standing out for some other reason.

Our need to be accepted is such a deep and primal instinct that we will even adopt attitudes and behaviours contrary to our own values if it means we will belong and be accepted. What happens when someone is not accepted? It causes pain, anguish, stress, and other problems. For our hunter-gatherer ancestors, being left out of the group could even mean death.

That's powerful stuff.

Imagine if you could harness that power towards the delivery of your purpose or strategy. How would your business perform if your people expected high standards of behaviour from each other?

Defining organisational culture

Understanding our instinctive need to be accepted helps us define culture. It's …

The attitudes and behaviours people adopt to fit in with the expectations of the people around them.

Which is often shortened to:

The attitudes and behaviours people adopt to fit in.

I use this definition because it highlights two things:

- Culture is attitudes and behaviours. It's how people think, feel, and behave.

- We all share an instinctive habit of adopting the attitudes and behaviours of the people around us to fit in with their expectations.

Expectations are communicated through a variety of means, but the ones that have the most influence on culture are *stories, leaders, systems*, and *symbols*, or more specifically by the way we interpret, or are encouraged to interpret, stories, leaders, systems, and symbols.

In chapter 9 we look at how to work with them as part of your culture program. For now, we need to understand why they are so important.

The power of stories

We all love stories. We listen, watch, and re-tell them over and over. We talk about them, interpret them, and take meaning from them.

As a species we've used stories for centuries as a way of educating, influencing, and shaping attitudes. Stories are a core influencing technique. How often do you use an example, or tell a story, to try to win an argument?

Stories are used to shape the way we think. People will not only share a story, they will use it as an example of how they think, and how they expect us to think.

A while ago I was conducting a cultural assessment for a construction company using focus groups. I asked one group about the management of the company, and one person became very angry and upset about an incident that had happened six months earlier. The whole crew had given up their weekend to complete a project, and one individual even missed his daughter's birthday party. They had sacrificed on behalf of the company – and when it was all over not one manager had said thank you.

He was angry. He thumped his fist on the table in frustration at how they were treated after they had given so much.

Later, I discovered this person had only been with the company for *three* months.

It wasn't his story. He wasn't working there and had not been affected by the incident.

But, he had heard it over and over as an example of how the 'management' of the company behaved. The people telling him the story expected him to be as upset as they were, and he obliged. He responded by getting angry even though it hadn't directly affected him.

That's the power of stories.

At roughly the same time I was working with another construction company where the workers told each other stories about the buildings they had completed, how great they looked, how safe they were, and the pride they felt when they drove past them and thought about what they had achieved.

What stories are people sharing in your organisation and what expectations are they communicating?

The importance of leadership

We all know the massive impact leadership has on culture. People will interpret a leader's expectations based on that leader's actions and then adapt their behaviour to fit in with those perceived expectations. This can be challenging because it means people are making assumptions about what their leader wants.

The age-old expression 'actions speak louder than words' is especially true for the actions of leaders. If a leader constantly pushes for productivity and doesn't ask questions about safety or reinforce safe practices, people will assume he or she expects them to prioritise productivity over safety and they will cut corners to get things done more quickly.

This places a great responsibility on leaders to be aware of the unspoken messages their actions are communicating. Leaders need to be authentic and make sure their expectations are clear and consistent with their actions because the culture will be shaped by the way people interpret their actions.

The value of systems

Organisations create systems in the form of processes, procedures and structured activities to drive specific behaviours. These systems help to communicate the expectations of the company.

If a system makes sense and is supported by the culture it will influence behaviour. People will adopt the desired behaviour.

If a system does not make sense and is not supported, people will find a way around it.

For systems to be successful they need to be supported by the culture.

The influence of symbols

Symbols and symbolic gestures can have a very powerful effect on attitudes and behaviours.

They are challenging because you can't control how people will interpret them. Have you ever tried to acknowledge someone for good work, only to have it backfire? They didn't appreciate the gesture, didn't think it was significant enough, or someone else asked why they didn't get the same thing?

Just about anything can have a symbolic impact: office size or location, desks, parking spaces, rewards, tokens of appreciation, gestures – the list is endless. The challenge is to understand what people see as symbolic and the expectations this communicates. It's a critical conversation to have in your business, and you will need to listen and accept what you hear.

Misleading definitions of culture

One of the reasons people struggle to understand culture is because the most common definitions of culture don't explain *how culture is created.* They talk about the *outcome* of culture, not the culture itself.

The two most commonly used definitions are:

- 'the way we do things around here' – the colloquial option.

- 'shared values, beliefs, and norms' – the dictionary option.

Neither captures our ability to instinctively adopt attitudes and behaviours, based on the expectations of the people around us, without realising it's happening. They define the outcome of that process, which is a consistent way of doing things and shared values, beliefs, and norms. As a result, people struggle to understand what culture really is. They understand that something is created but they don't understand the creation process.

To understand culture you need to understand how it is created.

A simple way to work with culture

Understanding how culture is created gives a fantastic clue to the easiest way to work with culture. You can *consciously* create it by talking about the attitudes and behaviours you need to be successful.

Make culture a *conscious* choice.

You can transform your organisation just by asking people to think about, and reflect on, their attitudes and behaviours, and the attitudes and behaviours needed to deliver the purpose and strategy of the organisation.

When you do this, culture becomes:

The attitudes and behaviours people consciously adopt to deliver the purpose and strategy of the organisation.

MAKING CULTURE
CONSCIOUS

You don't need to be an expert in culture, you just need to be willing to listen to their perspective and share your observations.

It can be that simple.

Chapter 2
Nine principles to guide you

'We control our actions, but the
consequences that flow from those actions
are controlled by principles.'

STEPHEN R. COVEY

Principles are defined as a 'natural law or fundamental truth'. They are like laws of nature, and they impact what you're doing whether you like it or not. For example, the principle of 'planning and preparation improves performance' exists whether you follow it or not. If you ignore this principle you will find it harder to be successful.

Life is easier when we follow principles

Contrary to popular belief, principles are *not* the same as values.

Values are a *choice*. You can decide what values you want to live by.

Principles exist *independently of you*, and will impact what you are doing whether you like it or not. Your choice is not what the principles are, but whether you decide to identify, understand, and follow them.

The hard part is identifying and understanding a principle. How do you know a principle exists? Are there principles affecting your business culture that you don't know about? Principles are not written down anywhere, so how do we figure them out?

You need to identify them for yourself.

Some are obvious; others require careful thought and observation.

Once you've made an observation about a situation, you need to decide if there is a principle at work. To be a principle, it must make sense and apply in any situation. For example, does the idea that 'planning and preparation improves performance' make sense and apply to any situation? If the answer is yes, it's probably a principle. The decision for you is then whether that principle is worth following.

Principles and your organisational culture

'Culture change' programs are so often harder than necessary because they work against natural principles. What follows in this chapter are nine principles that drive the A.D.A.P.T. process and will make your culture program much easier if you follow them. These principles are:

1. People commit to what they create.

2. Simple is best.

3. Proactive beats reactive.

4. Your people are your culture.

5. Everyone wants to be part of a great culture.

6. Each culture is unique.

7. Culture should be your highest priority.

8. Continuous improvement creates long-term success.

9. It should be easy.

Let's take a look …

People commit to what they create

People will be much more committed to a target culture if they have helped to create it. Imposing a culture *on* people is hard work, and unlikely to succeed. How would you feel if someone came to you and said, 'you must have *this* culture and we are going to measure it using *this* survey'?

This is what most companies are doing – and it's cultural insanity.

Simple is best

Why are people making culture so complicated? It doesn't need to be. If you keep it simple, you will get a better outcome. This is true for most things. The more you complicate it the harder it becomes.

Proactive beats reactive

This is a universal principle. The people who are proactively thinking about culture and taking action will get far better results than those who are always reacting to bad situations or a poor culture.

Your people are your culture

Instead of *telling* people what is needed, we should be *asking* them what is needed.

Your people live and breathe the culture every day. They experience every aspect, and understand how it impacts performance. You just need to trust them, talk to them (about the right things), listen to them, and they will help you create a *great* culture.

Everyone wants to be part of a great culture

If you understand and follow this principle, you will achieve magical results.

Do you really know anyone who doesn't want to be part of a great culture?

People will contribute to the process if you keep it simple and you are genuine about culture, committed to greatness, and humble enough to engage them in the process.

Each culture is unique

Each culture is full of unique people, in unique circumstances. What might work with one group could just as easily fail with another. That's why listening to your people is so important.

Only you and your people can create a great culture in your organisation.

It's crazy to think someone else, or a survey, or an app can tell you what your culture should be. That's a decision you and your team need to make.

It's also crazy to think someone else can create the culture for you. The idea of a consultant rolling out a program that will create an amazing culture might seem easy and appealing, but it's flawed. One wrong move from a leader and the whole program is wasted.

You and your leaders need to engage with your people to create a great culture.

Culture should be your highest priority

Culture has been identified as powerful enough to drive an individual to make decisions and take actions contrary to their own values and beliefs. That is extraordinary power.

As a leader, understanding how to create a great culture in which people expect and demand the right behaviour from each other should be your highest priority. If it's not, you are ignoring a powerful force and leaving the attitudes and behaviours in your business to be created by something or someone else.

Continuous improvement creates long-term success

This applies to any situation, but is especially true for culture.

The best results are achieved over time, and will include a lot of reviewing, reflection, continuous improvement and learning. This is why it needs to be a high priority.

You don't need to be an expert, you just need to be willing to listen, learn, correct your mistakes, and to work together.

It should be easy

If you are working against any of these principles, you are making life harder than it needs to be. If people feel involved in the culture and they understand and support it, the process will be easy.

* * *

The A.D.A.P.T. chapters in this book give you a process that will help you engage your people in defining a culture they will support and expect from each other.

Chapter 3
Meeting your employees' needs

Maslow's Hierarchy of Needs

You are probably familiar with Maslow's Hierarchy of Needs, as shown in the diagram over the page. It demonstrates that we cannot satisfy psychological needs like 'self-esteem' or 'belonging' if our physical needs such as food, shelter, and safety have not been met.

This makes sense. It would be hard to talk to someone about self-fulfilment if they hadn't eaten for two days.

Ross Judd's Hierarchy of Employee Needs

Maslow's concept can be translated to organisational culture, and helps us understand what employees need so they can help create a great organisational culture.

Security needs

The most basic needs Maslow identified were physiological, meaning the things we need to survive, like food, water, and shelter.

In terms of organisational culture, the survival requirements are salary and job security. If they are threatened we *feel like* our survival is threatened. It's not a logical or rational response; clearly someone wouldn't die if they lost their job. It's a neurological response based on deep instincts. We will still go to work if these things are threatened, but we won't be able to think as clearly, or make good decisions.

You will find it very difficult to talk to people about culture if they are worried they will lose their job and not be able to pay their mortgage, buy groceries, and satisfy their 'survival' needs. And yet, how many companies have enacted redundancies and then immediately imposed a 'culture change' program? Are they really expecting people to contribute positively to the business's culture when they are wondering if there will be another round of redundancies and if they will still have a job in a month?

And what happens if a leader behaves in a way that causes people to feel their job is threatened?

People need to *feel* secure; if they don't, everything else is hard work.

Safety needs

The next level is safety. In organisations, this is physical and psychological safety.

People will not participate in improving the culture if they feel their safety is threatened, meaning they feel like they are working in unsafe conditions or there will be repercussions if they speak up.

Leaders need to create a safe place to work if they want to build a culture where people demand and expect the right behaviours from each other.

MASLOW'S HIERARCHY OF NEEDS	ROSS JUDD'S HIERARCHY OF EMPLOYEE NEEDS
Fulfilling potential & creative needs — **SELF ACTUALISATION**	Achieving full potential Innovation & Opportunities
A feeling of Accomplishment — **ESTEEM**	Achieving something meaningful
Relationships Love Friends — **BELONGING**	Strong work relationships Trust Respect
Safe from Threats — **SAFETY**	Safe from Injury, Free to speak up
Food Shelter Survival — **PHYSIOLOGICAL**	Salary Security

27

Psychological needs: belonging and self-esteem

The next two levels are psychological, and won't be achieved if people feel like their security or safety is threatened.

People need to belong to something worthwhile or meaningful. In organisations, this is experienced as loyalty to the company, a sense of belonging to a team, project, site or company, and feeling that work has meaning.

People will be loyal to a company if they feel secure and safe, but feelings of self-esteem will be enhanced by engaging them in a conversation about the purpose of the company and the culture needed to deliver that purpose.

Any time you connect people with a purpose, you are creating a deeper meaning for their work and they will feel a strong sense of belonging and self-esteem.

Self-fulfilment needs: self-actualisation

The final level is self-actualisation. This is a state in which people relax and perform to their full potential. They are often more creative, innovative and successful.

Maslow's Hierarchy makes it clear this is only possible when people feel secure, safe, and part of a team that is doing something meaningful.

That makes sense. It's hard to achieve your full potential if you are worried about things like putting food on the table, repercussions if you speak up, or whether you are accepted by your leader and team.

A strong culture is the essential ingredient that helps people achieve their full potential. People are more creative when they feel the team will accept and explore their crazy ideas, or when they feel like they are doing something meaningful. If people feel threatened they withdraw and will only do what they are told.

Leadership principles

This hierarchy establishes a set of principles that leaders need to understand and follow to build a positive culture in their organisation:

1. People need to *feel* secure.

2. People need to *feel* safe to speak up.

3. You need to build healthy relationships that create a sense of belonging.

4. People need to have a sense of purpose and feel their work is meaningful.

5. Then you will find it much easier to engage people in creating a culture that will help them achieve their full potential.

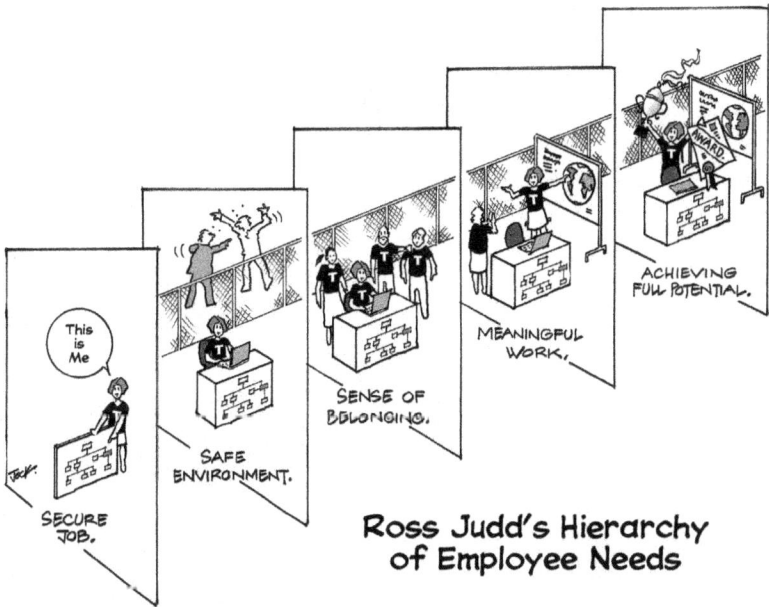

Ross Judd's Hierarchy of Employee Needs

Chapter 4
10 common culture mistakes to avoid

Due to the many scandals across all types of institutions in recent years, organisations have felt increased pressure to address and improve their culture. But mistakes are being made that will limit results and make improvements harder to achieve. Instead of following the principles in chapter 2, businesses are implementing crazy processes and complicating the issue.

10 common mistakes

In this chapter we'll look at the 10 biggest mistakes I often see businesses make when trying to overhaul their internal culture.

Being reactive instead of proactive

Initiating a culture program because something has gone wrong, or you received a bad score from an engagement survey, or you are frustrated, is a common mistake, and violates the principle, 'you will be more effective if you are proactive instead of reactive'.

It's a poor way to start a culture program because you are starting from the premise that something is wrong.

The proactive approach is to think about culture as part of your strategic planning process. Including a conversation about the culture needed to deliver your purpose and strategy is a very effective way of involving your whole company in a positive conversation designed to create a great culture that will deliver success to the business.

It's a mistake to build a strategy without including culture. You need to state your purpose (why you exist), what you want to achieve (your strategy), and how you will achieve it through both the strategic actions *and* culture.

This is a positive and powerful approach.

A strategy can have all the clever ideas you like, but none of that matters if it's not executed. Talking to your people about the attitudes and behaviours needed to deliver the strategy engages people with the execution of the strategy.

It's easy to do. Talk to your people about your purpose and strategy and ask for their input on the type of culture needed to deliver it. The more you listen, the clearer it will become. If you don't build this conversation into your strategy you are leaving the culture open to interpretation and influence from other factors, which can lead to disastrous results.

Most companies are really good at the strategic actions but ignore culture until it's too late.

Don't make that mistake.

Assuming values are enough

Listing a set of corporate values doesn't build a culture.

Can you remember your corporate values? How meaningful are they?

Values only work if you talk about them often enough for people to understand and apply them. In most companies that doesn't happen. They are placed on a wall and forgotten.

This happens because they are too complicated.

Most companies create four, five or even six values and then explain each one with sub-values or behavioural expectations. It's unrealistic to think people will remember them.

This approach rarely creates the desired culture. It's far more effective to describe your culture in simple terms so people can talk about it easily. The more they talk about it, the more meaningful and effective it will become.

Equating culture with happiness

This mistake stems from a poor understanding of culture, and guarantees mediocrity.

People seem to think that if 'there are no problems,' or, 'everything is fine,' or, 'people get along', the culture must be good. But 'getting along' is just one component of culture; it's not a defining characteristic, and it's certainly not a guarantee that you have a great culture.

In the example of the retail store in the introduction, the attitude and behaviour was 'let things go', which led to poor performance and a messy store. The staff were probably happy, getting along, and feeling good, but the store was a mess and customers were ignored.

Imposing culture change

Too many companies are mandating a culture change program, which violates the principle 'people commit to what they create'.

It also stifles engagement, because the minute you mention 'change' it suggests something is wrong, and the minute you suggest something is wrong people become defensive, and the minute people become defensive you've lost the opportunity to have a positive conversation with them.

It's far more powerful to explore culture as part of strategy.

IMPOSING CULTURE.

Delegating accountability for culture

You cannot delegate accountability for culture to renamed HR departments – the 'People and Culture' department – or an external consultant. Leaders are accountable for culture.

HR, or People and Culture, can be a fantastic resource, and can be held accountable for providing services and support to leaders to develop a great culture, but they cannot be held accountable for the resulting culture. This is the accountability of the leaders in the business.

Using climate or engagement surveys to assess culture

Climate or engagement surveys are not designed to assess culture – they are designed to assess the levels of engagement in your people.

Using them as an indicator of culture is a mistake because you will only get insight into how people are feeling; you won't get insight into their general attitudes and behaviours. In other words, you will only get insight into one specific attitude – which is whether people are engaged and intend to stay with the organisation.

The staff in the retail store example might have reported as happy and intending to stay in a climate survey, but their attitudes and behaviours towards a tidy store and customer engagement were clearly sub-standard.

A better option is to assess your culture using a qualitative approach, or interviews and focus groups. Good assessors can follow threads and develop a great understanding of the unique attitudes and behaviours in the business.

Putting 'band aids' on culture

A strong culture is not built through team-building activities or a new coffee machine in the lunch room. It needs to be part of your strategic planning process and a key accountability of leaders.

Refusing to engage an external perspective

It's almost impossible to get an accurate perspective when you are part of the culture. This is because you will have adopted the attitudes and behaviours of the group.

You will need an external perspective.

Letting your external partner do too much

Only you and your leaders can create a great culture. The idea of someone 'fixing this mess for you' might seem appealing but it's not realistic. You and your leaders need to lead the process that develops your culture, not someone else.

Getting the balance right between not engaging an external partner at all (which is a mistake) and engaging with them too much (which is also a mistake) is discussed further in chapter 12, 'Engaging an external partner'.

Over-complicating the process

You don't need complex surveys, convoluted definitions, mountains of data, charts, graphs, or anything else to build a great culture. Over-complicating the process is one of the biggest mistakes being made. Culture is a natural and intuitive process that should follow natural and intuitive principles.

Chapter 5
The cure for the cultural insanity

A.D.A.P.T. is the cure for the cultural insanity.

It follows the principles in this book and avoids significant mistakes. It's proactive because you are starting with purpose. It doesn't mandate a culture because it engages people in defining the culture needed to deliver the purpose. It keeps things simple and easy to understand, and leaders facilitate the whole process so you are creating your own culture.

Here is the A.D.A.P.T. framework:

Align with purpose *(see chapter 6)*

Define target culture *(see chapter 7)*

Assess current culture *(see chapter 8)*

Plan *(see chapter 9)*

Transform *(see chapter 9)*

It's extremely powerful and effective for transforming culture.

Understanding levels of change

A.D.A.P.T. is based on a theory from Robert Dilts, a renowned change therapist and organisational psychologist. He developed a very useful model that helps us understand levels of change.

I've modified his model slightly by placing it into an iceberg to convey the idea of 'deeper' levels.

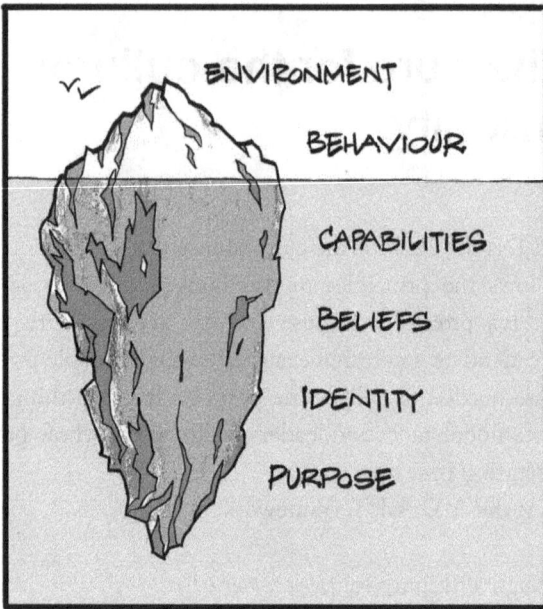

Dilts identified that change only occurs when you work two levels deeper than the issue you are trying to address. This means that if you want to change behaviour, you need to change the *belief that drives the behaviour*.

If you want to learn a new skill or capability, you need to see yourself differently, or create a new identity. At the very least, you would need to see yourself as someone who needs those skills or capabilities.

A deeper transformation

A full transformation occurs when you make a change at the deepest level.

When you redefine your purpose, or your reason for doing what you are doing, you will automatically create a new identity, which will drive a new set of beliefs, which will create new skills, behaviours, and environment.

This is why the A.D.A.P.T. process is so powerful. You first engage with people to **A**lign with a purpose that will trigger the deepest level of transformation.

It will create a new identity because people will start to see themselves differently.

When you have the conversation to **D**efine the target culture, you will bring that identity to life. This will drive new beliefs, skills, behaviours, and environment.

A roadmap for greatness

The A.D.A.P.T. process is deliberately designed to overcome the most common mistakes and create something different, exciting, and motivating for everyone in the organisation.

It will overcome the approaches that lead to mediocrity, and engages you in a simple process that can lead to greatness.

Look through the items in the checklist on the next two pages and ask yourself where your answers 'land'. If your answers are closer to the left side of the checklist then you are currently using an approach that will be hard work and deliver mediocre results.

If you need to move towards the right side of the checklist then you are in the right place. The following chapters outline the A.D.A.P.T. process and provide a roadmap to take you there.

MEDIOCRITY ←——

I am initiating a culture program because of a problem ←——

We have a poor definition & don't understand 'culture' ←——

I am violating sound principles and making it hard ←——

We are talking in vague terms about 'culture' ←——

Our starting premise is that there's a problem ←——

I have mandated a culture program ←——

We have a vague target to 'improve' our culture ←——

A leader, consultant or survey has defined our target culture ←——

My leaders are telling people what the culture should be ←——

I have assessed our current culture with a complicated survey ←——

I have experts planning our culture program ←——

I have engaged an external partner that tells me what to do ←——

I am telling my people what is needed ←——

I am finding this hard and complicated ←——

I am measuring results with complicated assessment tools ←——

HR or People and Culture are accountable for the results ←——

This process is hard work ←——

➡ GREATNESS

→ I am initiating a culture program as part of my strategic plan

→ We have defined culture as 'attitudes and behaviours'

→ I am following sound principles and keeping it simple

→ We are having conscious conversations about attitudes & behaviours

→ Our starting premise is to Align with Purpose

→ I have engaged my people in a culture program

→ We have a clearly defined target culture

→ My people have defined our target culture

→ My leaders are facilitating conversations about culture

→ I have assessed our current culture with interviews and focus groups

→ I have engaged people from my business to plan the culture program

→ I have engaged an external partner to listen & coach me on the process

→ I am trusting my people to tell me what is needed

→ I am enjoying a simple and intuitive process

→ I am measuring results with simple business measures that make sense

→ The leaders in my business are accountable for the results

→ The process is a lot of fun

A new definition of culture

When you implement the A.D.A.P.T. process, the definition of culture becomes:

> *The attitudes and behaviours people consciously discuss, adopt, and expect from each other to deliver the purpose and strategy of the organisation.*

Imagine that.

Imagine your people consciously talking about and creating a culture that will deliver success. Instead of pushing a big blob of jelly up a hill, you are now getting the jelly to decide how it will get there. The jelly then will absorb you and take you with it.

This is the ultimate experience, and something every organisation, team, or group should aspire to achieve.

Over the next four chapters we will look at each step in the A.D.A.P.T. framework.

Chapter 6
Align with purpose

The best company cultures are driven by purpose. A clear and compelling purpose gives meaning, direction, and a strong reason for working.

It touches the soul.

You should consider your culture as part of your vision and strategy, but to truly inspire your people, the heart of your culture must be your purpose. Strategy is more business oriented – it's important, but it doesn't have the same emotional connection or effect. If you are focusing your culture around strategy you can build a good culture. Aligning with purpose builds a *great* culture.

Think about it this way: a good builder will build a house based on a plan and strategy. They will follow the plan and put the house together correctly. It will be safe, weatherproof, and a nice house to live in.

A *great* builder will have a deeper purpose – it might be something like 'to create a great living space'. They will also follow a plan that will build a safe, weatherproof house, but their purpose will cause them to look for extra touches and make suggestions that will make the final product great to live in.

The question is *why*

To build a compelling purpose, you need to answer the question 'why?'

Why do we exist? *Why* do we do what we do?

For the builder, the question is 'why do we build houses?' And the answer needs to go beyond obvious things like 'to make money' or 'to give people somewhere to live'.

The idea is to tap into a purpose strong enough to create a compelling motivation for new attitudes and behaviours.

Here are some examples.

Community safety

In 2009 I had the privilege of working with a group of prison officers. The obvious reason for their existence was to keep prisoners locked up, but as we discussed it further they came to realise they existed to keep the community safe, which they summarised as 'community safety'.

This gave new meaning to their work. They started to think about how they could return honest, reliable, safe, respectful, and decent citizens to the community, which then got them thinking about how they role-modelled those attitudes and behaviours.

They decided to focus on respect, and their catch cry became, 'If prisoners don't learn respect from us, who will they learn it from?'

You can imagine the shift in attitudes and behaviours. They quickly created a workplace where they expected respect from each other and you had to demonstrate respect to fit in. They told each other stories about how important it was to respect each other and role model that respect to the prisoners.

It became a great place to work, and had a positive impact on the prisoners as well.

Supporting industry

Another group that I worked with ran the only glass 'floatline' in Australia. This is what they call the production line that melts sand and makes glass. It's called a floatline because the melting sand 'floats' on other molten materials as they create the thickness and colour they need.

Their obvious purpose is to make glass, and yet once again, as we continued the conversation, they realised they exist to support the glass-processing industry in Australia. This is an industry full of small businesses that buy the raw, unprocessed glass, and put the finishing touches on it like cutting it to size, making double-glazed windows, and toughening and polishing the glass.

This industry could buy its raw glass from overseas, but the glass made in Australia was easier to source, cheaper, and better quality. Smaller businesses could buy small amounts at short notice, instead of needing to order a container three months in advance from overseas.

They were a very important supplier that added value to an industry which employed a lot of people.

This new purpose created new attitudes and behaviours. Suddenly the glass workers became concerned about the customer. Where they had previously forgotten about the glass once it left their factory, they now started thinking about its condition and the customer's experience when it arrived. They started visiting customers, and discovered that simple, small changes made a huge difference when the glass was delivered.

More examples

A school took their purpose well beyond the idea of 'educating students' and realised their school played an important function in the development of the whole individual and in the community. They called it 'life support', which they knew sounded corny but it had rich meaning for them.

An accounting firm went beyond the idea of providing accounting, finance, wealth management, and auditing services and realised they existed to create successful businesses. They called it 'shared success'.

A mining company went beyond the idea of drawing minerals from the ground and understood the delicate balancing act they played in supporting small rural communities, environmental management, and profitably providing minerals that support the modern urban lifestyle. They decided they existed to 'sustainably support all communities', which they summarised as 'supporting communities'.

The glue that binds

You need a compelling purpose if you want to build a great culture, *and* if you get the purpose right it will almost build the culture for you because it will drive the attitudes and behaviours you need. It's the glue that brings individuals, teams, departments, and companies together.

We all know that a common goal is the defining characteristic of a great team. Alignment to a deep and compelling purpose is the defining characteristic of a *great* culture. It's the foundation on which greatness is built.

If you build your culture on anything else you are building a foundation for mediocrity.

Creating a new identity

Just this step on its own can create a dramatic transformation in your organisation because people will shift their attitudes and behaviours to deliver a compelling purpose.

The neurological explanation is that it creates a new identity.

Identity is how we see ourselves, or feel about ourselves. If we see ourselves differently then we will behave differently. As the prison officers focused on 'community safety' their identity shifted from 'guards' to 'role models'. They brought this to life by deciding to focus their culture on 'respect'.

The glassworkers shifted from people who made glass to people who supported a thriving industry in Australia, which in turn created different expectations, attitudes, and behaviours.

Cascading conversations

These conversations need to happen throughout the entire organisation. It's not something that senior executives discuss and then 'tell' the rest of the business. It's a conversation each leader, at every level, needs to have with their team, department, division, site, or section.

It starts at the top and cascades through the organisation.

The steps to creating and implementing a strong purpose

The first step is to create the purpose for the whole company. To do this the CEO, GM, or another leader will gather a group of people together for the 'why' discussion.

There are two options for the people they bring together:

- their executive or leadership team

- a representative sample of people from across the company.

The advantage of the first option is the executive team are all engaged in the process and will have a stronger commitment to the outcome. The advantage of the second option is that it sends a clear message about engagement and involvement, and brings greater diversity and experience to the conversation.

Whichever option they choose, the outcome needs to be a clear purpose, or *why this company exists*. It will be something meaningful that touches people at a deep and personal level.

The next step is even *more important*.

Each leader in the business must now mirror that conversation with their department, area, division, site, or team, and this process needs to cascade throughout the entire company.

Here is a hypothetical example. Let's imagine the CEO of a car manufacturer and their executive team decide they exist for 'safe experiences'. To them, this means that every car they produce safely contributes to life's experiences.

Their motto might become 'providing life's experiences', because when someone buys a car it will become a major contributor to many of their experiences.

The different leaders in the business would need to talk to their teams about what that means for them:

- The head of 'sports cars' would discuss why they build sports cars in the context of providing safe experiences. What type of experience does a sports car create? How does it contribute to the overall purpose of 'safe experiences'? They might decide they provide 'driving experiences' and design cars that are fantastic to drive that also include all the safety technology. They might adopt 'driving experiences' as the moto for their division.

- The head of 'SUVs' would discuss why they build SUVs. What type of experiences do they create? They might decide to focus on 'family experiences', and build features into their SUVs that support that purpose.

- The CFO would talk to their team about how they managed the finances of the business to support the delivery of 'safe experiences'. They might opt for something like 'safe and secure finances'.

The point is that each leader will create a unique purpose for their team in the context of the overall company purpose.

Alignment is more important that uniformity

You might be thinking, 'won't we end up with a bunch of different purposes?'

Yes and no.

Yes, because they will all sound a little different as they will use their own language. *No*, because they have all been discussed, agreed, and aligned in the context of the overall company purpose. In other words they are all created to support the company purpose.

Alignment is the most critical part, and is more important than having one 'uniform' purpose.

Consider the alternative. Do you really think you can come up with one statement that will give meaning and motivation for every division, department, team, site, or individual? It's far more powerful for each leader to have a conversation with their team about how they are aligned with the company purpose.

Imagine that.

Every team in your business focusing on a purpose that's unique and meaningful for them because it will deliver the overall company purpose.

That would be a special place to work.

Chapter 7
Define target culture

One word

Once your organisation is aligned to its purpose, the next step is to define a target culture.

This is a fantastic conversation because it will get your whole company thinking about the attitudes and behaviours needed to 'fit in' and deliver the purpose of the organisation.

Your objective is to define the target culture in *one word*.

Yes, one word. Okay, two at the most.

Most people react to this idea by thinking it's not possible or it won't work as a way of building a culture.

The opposite is true. It *is* possible – and it works brilliantly.

Simplicity

It works because it keeps things simple and conscious.

Your people are your culture, so you need to be able to consciously discuss the target culture in the simplest terms possible. Getting to one word makes that possible.

Let's look at the current alternative. Almost every organisation on the planet defines their culture with a set of four, five or even six values, and then, in most cases, they have expanded definitions of each.

It seems like a thorough and comprehensive way to define a target culture. But is it working?

Can you remember *your* company values? Can your people? Do they influence your behaviour? How often do you talk about them with someone else at work? How often does your leader talk to you about the company values?

For most people the reality is: *it's all too much*.

There is only so much we can retain in our conscious minds at one time. Neuroscientists talk about '$7^{\pm2}$', which is just a clever way of saying the most you can retain at any time is nine things. If you came to work worried about an argument with your partner, and you are struggling with your personal finances, and something happened on the way to work that annoyed you, and your boss said something you didn't understand, and you are thinking about the project you are working on, and you need to return some emails, and you are not sure if the company is going to do another round of redundancies, you have limited capacity left in your conscious mind to think about culture. And for most of us that's a normal day.

It's unwise to think people will remember four or more values on top of all the other information that occupies their conscious mind during their working day. If you want to have any chance of people remembering and talking about culture, you need to summarise it in *one word*. (Or, maybe two.)

One word makes it possible to engage people in conversations that will continually shape attitudes and behaviours.

It's about the conversations

Before they have tried it, people often tell me this is *too* simple. They think one word couldn't *possibly* capture everything that's needed when you define culture.

That is correct – and it's also missing the point.

You are not trying to accurately describe everything that's needed in one word; you are trying to *start and maintain a conversation*. The conversation is far more important than the definition, and using one word makes it much easier to have the conversation.

So let's have a look at the two different ways you can get to your one word.

Getting to one word (or two): purpose-driven option

The most popular approach to facilitate the conversation to identify one word is to have the conversation about purpose and target culture at the same time. It makes sense. You bring a group of people together to explore the purpose of the organisation, and as part of the conversation you discuss the culture needed to deliver that purpose. It's a seamless approach, with the advantage that it's heavily influenced by the thinking and discussion that has gone into the conversation on purpose.

It also makes sense because a new identity will emerge as you discuss your purpose. Moving straight into defining your target culture will bring that identity to life.

Let's examine a hypothetical example.

A small accounting firm decides to re-examine why they exist. They might talk about their current service offering, clients, and what they really want to achieve. During the conversation the idea of helping their clients achieve financial freedom continues to emerge. Each time it emerges they dismiss the idea because it's too extreme. They make comments like, 'we can't do that because we don't provide wealth management services', or, 'our people don't take a holistic approach; they are too focused on their area of expertise'.

But as they continue the discussion, they realise they find the idea deeply motivating. It creates a passion they hadn't experienced before.

They have discovered their purpose, and they've already thought about the attitudes and behaviours they would need to deliver that outcome. Each time they dismissed the idea they were actually identifying something they would need, like a more holistic approach, thinking beyond their technical expertise, thinking about what else the client needs, and providing wealth management services.

They are *already well on their way to identifying a target culture.*

The next step is to identify the attitudes and behaviours people need to achieve those outcomes. It might be an attitude of 'holistic', or 'full service', or 'complete service', or 'combined service'.

Which is their best option?

The one that will prompt conversations about the culture they need to deliver their purpose.

Imagine an accounting firm talking about 'full service' or 'combined service'. Is it possible they would behave differently compared to other accounting firms, and that their culture would become a point of difference and a competitive advantage?

Getting to one word (or two): overcoming challenges option

Another way to facilitate the conversation to identify the 'word' is to think about the challenges you will face in achieving your purpose. Ask questions like:

- What hurdles, challenges, or issues will we need to overcome to achieve our purpose?

- What attitudes and behaviours will we need to overcome those hurdles?

Again, as you explore the attitudes and behaviours, a theme will emerge and you will be able to summarise the target culture with one word, or two at the most.

Five tips for finding the one word

Tip one: an external consultant will add value to this conversation, but be very careful about who you engage. You need someone who has zero attachment to your content and outcome. The minute the facilitator thinks they have the answer for you *they are no longer useful.*

A good facilitator will listen carefully to the group and identify the patterns that are emerging. They will notice which comments carry more 'energy' or 'enthusiasm', and guide the group to recognise those comments.

The second tip is to keep track of the comments and ideas being expressed. Have someone capture them on a flip chart or screen that everyone can see. As ideas are being captured, people will start to notice a pattern, and that pattern will guide you to the word.

The third tip is to avoid perfection at all costs! You don't need to come up with the perfect word. All you need is a word that will get leaders talking to their teams. Sometimes the best option is the word that needs explanation, or seems like a challenging idea.

The fourth tip is to remember you can always change it. Quite often a group will choose a word that's a stepping stone to the culture they would ideally like. This often happens if the culture is too aspirational.

The fifth, and biggest, tip is to trust the group. They will know what is needed. Listen and take note of what they are saying. Your people are your culture.

Some examples

Here are some examples drawn from my experience.

The prison officers who identified 'community safety' as their purpose initially chose 'support' as their culture because they acknowledged that supporting each other was their biggest challenge. Their current culture was 'toxic'. They focused on support as the first step towards their ultimate target of 'respectful'. It took a few years, but eventually they shifted their focus to 'respect'.

I worked with a group of auditors. They worked for, and audited, the public service. The new Auditor General worked with them to identify 'improving the public service' as their purpose. This shifted them from thinking about themselves as 'auditors' or 'gatekeepers' to being a professional support function. They now audited to improve, not to find fault.

They chose 'professional' as their target culture. It had rich meaning for them around the way they worked and interacted with the public service and the behaviour they role-modelled both internally and externally.

Another company was spread across Australia and was riddled with issues. Product was never delivered on time, people never honoured their commitments, and the company was making a loss.

The executive team established an ambitious strategy to turn around their performance, and realised it would fail if people did not honour their commitments. They chose a culture of 'achievement' – which to them meant 'we do what we say we will do'.

Another group had recently merged with their competitor. They had ended up with roughly 50% of people from each 'side' of the merger. They were not delivering on their commitments, and their manager wanted a culture along the lines of 'accountable' or 'achievement'.

We held an offsite with a representative sample of people from the company and deliberately chose people who were 'influential', which is a nice way of saying outspoken and opinionated. The target culture chosen was 'engaged', because they hadn't properly engaged with each other since the merger. There were people who hadn't even said hello in six months! The group knew they needed to engage before they could start talking about 'accountability' or 'achievement'.

They were right.

Trust your people.

Another example was a retailer with stores in high-traffic areas like railway stations and airports. They sold small items like magazines, books, and other fast-moving consumer goods. When I explored their purpose, it took a while to get past 'making money', mainly because they couldn't see a deeper reason for their existence.

They eventually settled on 'convenience'. They existed to make the lives of their customers more convenient. Most customers were buying something at a time that was stressful, to make a journey more tolerable. The thing they were buying would make their lives a little more pleasant or 'convenient' during their trip.

They also realised the customer just wanted to deal with someone responsive – someone who understood they were in a hurry and didn't feel the need to ask them their life's story in the name of 'customer service'. They settled on 'responsive' as their culture.

Another group was spread across New Zealand. The biggest challenge they identified was getting their sites to work together. They chose 'one team'.

Another retail group was in a very competitive market and realised the only way to differentiate themselves was through their service. They chose 'customer centric'.

Another site was riddled with trust issues. They chose 'trust and respect' because it was desperately needed before they could do anything else.

A wholesaler had rebuilt their business and chose 'teamwork' in recognition of their need to work together more effectively to take the next step in their growth.

* * *

Your objective when you define your target culture is to identify a word that will get people *consciously talking about the culture*.

Each example above worked brilliantly because people kept talking about it. Leaders at all levels talked to their teams about how to be 'responsive' or 'professional'.

This is the power of one word. It gets people talking.

Stepping stones

This is a cascading conversation where alignment is more important that uniformity. Each leader in the business, at every level, needs to discuss with their team the culture they need to deliver the company purpose.

Quite often a team will recognise they need a different culture as a stepping stone to the ultimate target company culture. This is great because it means they understand and support the company culture *and want to get there*.

In the examples above, the group that chose 'engaged' recognised that was their most immediate need, and once they had engaged they could move on to the culture their GM wanted, which was accountability or achievement. They embraced the idea of 'engaged' and started talking to their leaders and other teams about how to engage. They also asked their leaders to spend more time on the shop floor, giving them updates on the business.

How fantastic is that?

Don't make the mistake of trying to drive the same culture throughout the entire organisation. You need to trust your leaders and their teams to *align* with your organisational culture. When they do they will develop a deeper understanding of the target culture. An organisation full of teams that are *aligned* to one culture is very effective and successful.

Chapter 8
Assess current culture

How to conduct effective assessments

The A.D.A.P.T. approach emphasises the importance of healthy conversations, and they are especially important when you are assessing your current culture.

There is no better way to understand attitudes and behaviours than by listening to people, which means interviews and focus groups. Too many people choose surveys because they appear faster, cheaper, and provide a numeric result or 'measure' the culture. The problem is they generate conversations about statistics, interpretation, and definitions instead of attitudes and behaviours. As a result, they are a false economy.

You will get much more from your people if you listen to their stories, gather their perspectives on leadership, assess how systems are driving behaviour, and understand the things they find symbolic. A skilled assessor will be able to achieve all this and more. They will follow threads and identify themes. They will read the group and interpret their verbal and non-verbal messages. They will also derive meaning from what people *don't* say.

You end up with a much more thorough understanding of your organisational culture.

The reason this approach is so effective is because a skilled assessor will develop a deeper understanding of the unique issues in your organisation. They will take note of the quiet comments people make and draw out more information. They will observe when someone is hesitating or deciding *not* to answer a question, and draw them into a conversation. Most of all, they will listen to the stories and build an understanding of the attitudes and behaviours in the business.

A skilled assessor will also interpret meaning. They are listening to more than just the comments – they are trying to understand the attitude, mindset, and beliefs that are driving those comments.

Uncovering themes

Interviews and focus groups achieve three things:

- they send a very clear message that you are taking a different approach and will engage people in the conversation
- they engage people
- they will uncover the consistent themes, ideas, and messages in the current culture, which can provide powerful insight.

As part of the process, a skilled assessor will look past the personal issues that individuals raise. For example, if someone has a strong opinion that's not supported by anyone else then their opinion will be noted but will usually be left out the final assessment of the attitudes in the business.

People are given the opportunity to talk and be heard, and that is something everyone craves. If you subscribe to the idea that culture is the attitudes and behaviours people adopt to fit in with the stories, leadership, systems, and symbols of the organisation then you need to talk to people and listen to their stories.

If you want to know what I think, come and talk to me.

The many problems with surveys

You can try using surveys, but how often have you conducted a survey and then debated, at length, what people meant by their answers?

Lies, damned lies, and statistics

Surveys provide statistics, and statistics create cynicism. You've probably heard expressions like 'there are three types of lies: lies, damned lies, and statistics'. Most people have a deeply rooted cynicism towards statistics and believe they can be manipulated. The net result is that people end up having unhealthy and unproductive conversations.

Strangely, one of the main reasons people use surveys is *because* they deliver a statistical answer. You get a number you can measure against in the future. Some surveys will even tell you the percentage your culture has improved since the last survey.

Really?

That might sound appealing, but think about it … do you really want to try to turn your culture into a number and then use that number in performance measures?

It's an unhealthy approach.

We're talking about culture. The attitudes and behaviours people adopt to fit in. You should be talking about attitudes and behaviours – not statistical measures.

Limited scope

Surveys are limited to the questions they were designed to assess. This means that if the designer is unaware of an issue it will never be included in a survey. You can try adding a 'general comments' section to capture additional information, but do they really work? Most of the time they raise questions that can't be answered.

Think about when you have filled out a customer satisfaction survey. Did it ask the right questions?

Add to that 'survey fatigue' and it's highly likely a survey will give you false or misleading data. The more surveys people are asked to complete the more they hurry or even fabricate their answers, just to be done with it.

There's also the possibility the current culture will influence how people fill out the surveys. If leaders are being measured on the results of a survey, they may consciously or unconsciously put pressure on people to give the 'right' answers.

Another potential issue is that survey questions prompt people to think about a certain topic. For example, I was conducting interviews and focus groups in a company that prided itself on being customer focused, and yet not one person talked about the customer. It was a tough message for the business. People were thinking about everything *but* the customer. If we had used a survey we would have asked a question about 'customer focus', and I'm sure it would have received a positive response. People were good at talking about the customer *when asked*, but it wasn't on their mind at other times. Customer focus was clearly not an attitude that was driving the culture.

You get what you measure

You've probably heard the expression 'you get what you measure'.

If you are using a survey to measure culture, it will drive the behaviour of the organisation towards achieving a better score in the survey. People will focus on the behaviours the survey measures and make sure they improve in those areas.

That might be okay in the short term but it's a poor long-term strategy. What if you decide you have improved accountability and need to focus on innovation or creativity? Will you make changes to the survey?

A false economy

People perceive surveys as a fast and cheap way to involve the whole business.

On the surface that appears to be true, but are any savings worth it if they are providing incomplete, inaccurate or false data, or locking you into a measurement that loses relevance in the future? Or generating a conversation about the instrument rather than the culture? That ends up being a much greater cost to the business than any apparent saving in conducting the survey.

When you consider costs, you also must factor in the time spent interpreting the data. I've seen groups locked in endless debate interpreting statistics and trying to understand what people might have been thinking when they answered a question. It wastes time in pointless debate and is a poor return on investment.

The power of language

Language is powerful. It creates meaning and shapes the way people think. Learning the language of a group or culture will give you great insight into how those people communicate, which will help you understand their attitudes and behaviours. Through interviews and focus groups, you will learn the 'cultural language' inside your organisation.

This also gives you the opportunity to present your findings in simple and consistent language. Using the language of the workforce is particularly powerful when you are presenting the results. Presenting in their language saves a lot of time and engages them more. They will feel 'heard'.

Contrast this with the idea of learning the specific terms used in a survey and ask yourself whether you would prefer to spend time explaining the definitions from a survey or talking to people, in their language, about the current culture of the organisation?

One organisation I worked with used a mixture of surveys and interviews. The survey reported them as low on 'achievement', which it defined as setting and achieving clear goals. They were surprised because they had spent a lot of time carefully measuring their goals and couldn't understand why the score on 'achievement' was so low.

However, in the interviews and focus groups, their people had talked about how they were 'obsessive' about their measures to the point they lost sight of the goal. This created a very different conversation about the difference between achievement and being obsessive about measures.

Interviews and focus groups provide unique insights into the attitudes and behaviours in the business. They also allow you to use the language of the workforce when you are presenting the data, which can save a lot of time and engages people more. They feel heard.

The many advantages of interviews and focus groups

The benefits you get from engaging with your workforce in conversations about the current culture cannot be overstated. It sends a clear message about the approach you are taking to this complex idea of 'culture', and is far more likely to elicit helpful contributions.

Too many companies are imposing culture change from the top, and using surveys as the instrument of that change. It's cultural insanity. Your people are your culture, so you will get better results if you make it clear you are going to engage them in the process.

What to ask

If you are conducting interviews and focus groups, your objective is to listen. I'm often surprised how much talking people do when they are supposed to be asking questions and listening.

Ask open questions that encourage people to talk. Your questions should be geared towards four key areas: stories, leadership, systems, and symbols.

I've never used the same set of questions twice, mainly because I adapt my questions based on the unique characteristics of each culture. The questions are designed to stimulate a conversation. The aim is to get people talking.

Encourage people to contribute more with prompts like 'tell me more' or 'that's interesting, what else can you tell me about that?'

Interpreting the answers

A skilled assessor will interpret meaning from what people have said rather than accepting their comments at face value. For example, one of the questions I often ask is, 'what are your managers (or leaders) doing well?'

In one client I got absolutely *nothing* in response to that question. You could have heard a pin drop. I held focus groups with over 150 workers, and not one of them answered the question. I even prompted groups with comments like 'come on, there must be something your manager does well …'

I got nothing.

I also asked what their managers could do differently … and got a shopping list of grievances.

There were different ways to interpret this:

1. If I took the silence on face value then the managers were so bad there was nothing positive to report.

2. The stories, comments, and interpretations about managers were so consistent and strong in the organisation they coloured the view of every single worker.

3. There was a cultural expectation that prevented people saying anything positive about their manager, which meant people were not prepared to speak up in focus groups.

I'd met the managers in question and knew they had some redeeming qualities. I also refused to believe that not one manager on the whole site was doing anything well. Surely one of them was doing something right!

I assessed this response as a cultural phenomenon, meaning it was a mixture of points 2 and 3 above. People were jaundiced in their view and not prepared to say anything positive in front of their peers.

I presented the data back to the workforce as a 'jaundiced view'.

Not everyone agreed with me, so it stimulated an interesting conversation.

As a point of interest, I did a similar assessment at the same company two years later. This time I got a much more balanced set of answers. There were things their managers were doing well and still a lot of things they could do differently.

This is an example of how a skilled assessor interprets meaning rather than accepting the comments at face value.

Presenting the results

Any time you assess culture you *must* present the results. People have contributed to the process and deserve this courtesy.

Interviews and focus groups make this much easier. You don't need to explain the terms you are using, you can simply present the data in their language.

You may still surprise people because you are giving them feedback which will include your interpretation, but that will generate a great conversation about the culture, instead of conversations about statistics.

Some examples of cultural observations

Here are some examples of cultural observations taken from a wide variety of my clients:

- *Us and them:* this was their language for the clear divisions between areas of the business.

- *Toxic:* this was the word most commonly used to describe the culture.

- *Boys' club:* their language for a perception that people were promoted based on their relationships rather than merit. It was tough feedback for the leaders.

- *Competitive:* highlighting issues between departments. In this business people were competing for resources like materials, equipment, and staff.

- *Blame, excuses, and denial:* highlighting a lack of personal responsibility and a strong attitude of blaming others for issues instead of thinking about how you have contributed to them.

- *Jaundiced:* this word was not used by the group but summarised their view of their managers.

- *Fractured:* this was from a client where the various parts of the business were deliberately ignoring each other and in some cases sabotaging each other.

- *Insular:* this is how people described themselves and their relationships with other areas of the business.

- *Supportive:* this was from a business that enjoyed a great culture. They were very proud of how much they supported each other.

- *Safe:* this was from a site where they had implemented a strong safety culture and took special care to 'look out for each other.' They talked a lot about being safe and safe practices.

- *Committed:* this was from a company very committed to their product and purpose. It was a small start-up business faced with lots of hurdles. They talked about how committed they were.

Why it's the third step

It's more useful to assess your culture after you have aligned with purpose and defined the target culture. This is because you can conduct interviews and focus groups that will help you understand the current culture in relation to the target culture.

People often do the assessment as the first step. This can work and will add value, but if you wait till you know the purpose and target culture you can add more value by including questions that will help you understand the work needed to bridge the gap.

Also, if you do an assessment as your first step it means the first conversations you have with people will be to explain 'we're doing a culture program'. People will hear that as a culture 'change' program, which means you are now starting from a weaker position.

It's far more effective to make the first conversation about purpose. Don't even talk about culture, just make sure your organisation is aligned with purpose.

Then you can talk about a target culture and assess your current culture to help identify the gaps between where you are and where you want to be.

Then the next steps are to Plan and Transform.

Chapter 9
Plan and Transform

You have now aligned your organisation with its purpose, defined a target culture, and assessed your current culture using interviews and focus groups. You will have a great understanding of the attitudes and behaviours in the organisation.

It's time to plan a transformation.

Plan and Transform are the most intriguing and exciting steps. There's something fantastic about a group of people coming together to plan how they will build a great culture, and then executing the plan. It's a lot of fun.

Getting started

The best way to do this is to bring together a representative sample of people from across your business. Your objective is to create a plan that addresses the four key influences on culture, being the stories, leadership, systems, and symbols in the organisation.

You will need people from the various divisions, departments, leadership levels, areas, and teams. They need to be people the rest of the organisation trusts.

There's no perfect group size. It's a matter of what you are prepared to invest and how you intend to facilitate the conversation.

There is also no perfect approach. It varies depending on the size of your group, the issues that need to be addressed, and your facilitator.

The first step is to make sure everyone is aligned to the purpose and target culture. You need to ensure everyone in the room is working in the same direction. This is the context for the conversation. It reconnects people with why you are doing this.

You need to set a clear objective for the conversation. What do you hope to achieve?

You will then examine the data from your culture assessment (see chapter 8) and compare the results with your target culture. What are the biggest gaps? Where do you need to focus?

You can then debate and brainstorm the steps needed to bridge the gap between your current and target culture. Generate a bunch of ideas – make them as crazy as you like. Have some fun, be creative, and make sure you don't take yourselves too seriously.

When you are done, work through the ideas you have generated and identify the ones that are viable options. Discuss how you would achieve them and set up specific actions.

You now have a plan to transform your business.

Remember – keep it simple. You are doing a gap analysis, and developing a set of actions to close the gap. The people you have brought together will make great contributions and you will have plenty of opinions and information to work with.

The steps are:

1. Set the context – reconnect with your purpose and target culture.

2. Set clear outcomes.

3. Conduct a gap analysis between the current and target culture.

4. Brainstorm ideas to bridge that gap.

5. Identify viable options.

6. Set actions.

You are planning a way forward to create a *great* culture.

The drivers of culture

As we've looked at earlier in the book, any plan to create a great culture will need to work with the stories, leadership, systems, and symbols in the organisation.

The power of stories

Stories play a strong and influential role in creating culture. People take meaning from them.

Quite often a story will become what I call 'folklore', which simply means everyone talks about it and it has grown to a point of great significance. It defines or creates attitudes and behaviours.

For example, you will remember the example from chapter 1 of the worker angry about a situation that occurred before he had even started with the company. That situation had become 'folklore'. Everyone had talked about it to the point it affected people that weren't even there.

In another company, people kept talking about a previous manager and his behaviour. I didn't think much of it – until I was told he hadn't worked there for over 10 years! Stories about him were 'folklore' and affected how people interpreted the behaviour of their current managers.

You need to challenge the interpretation of stories and create new stories. It's not easy, but it is possible.

Reframing stories

The best way to challenge the interpretation of a story is by reframing it. Reframing is very simple. You just look for a different meaning or interpretation of a story.

To do this you can ask the group you have brought together to identify any stories that need to be 'reframed' as part of building a great culture. For example, I was on a site where people talked about how their manager never came to see them. They felt neglected, until one of them pointed out that the manager trusted them and didn't *need* to visit. They then assigned different meaning to the same behaviour, and went from feeling neglected to feeling appreciated.

It's powerful because it challenges attitudes and interpretations.

If you are attempting to reframe stories you will need to remember:

- You are reframing to build a new culture.

- It can't be done by managers. It can only be done by a group trusted by the organisation. This is a test of whether you have chosen the right 'representative sample'.

- To achieve a reframe the facilitator needs to ask questions like, 'what's a different interpretation?' The facilitator must *not* offer an interpretation; that needs to come from the group.

- If a leader, or a leadership group, tries to reframe a story it will come across as manipulation. It's critical the group – your representative sample – does the reframing.

Trust your people. They want to be part of a great culture, and will quickly grasp how their interpretations are impacting the culture if you give them that opportunity.

It can be a lot of fun. I've had groups talking about the different meanings people could take from a situation or story. The funniest examples are when someone complains about something, it gets reframed … and they find something else to complain about.

When you reframe stories you are developing the neurological ability to *choose* the meaning you derive from a situation. That is a wonderful, powerful, and very proactive thing to develop because it puts you in greater control of your reactions and emotions.

Creating new stories

Another approach is to ask your representative group to identify new stories that need to be shared as part of the new culture.

Quite often people are unaware of simple changes that occur. They may not notice the communication from one team to another, or how their manager engaged them in a decision instead of telling them, or how the company supported a staff member in a time of need. It's important the group identify these changes and talk about them with the rest of the organisation. This helps people notice the changes.

We have the neurological ability to completely ignore things if they are not part of our focus of attention. Our ability to completely miss things because they are not 'on our radar' is astonishing, which means it's critical to highlight and discuss the changes that are taking place as they happen. If you don't, people will miss them. Bring them to people's attention so they become the stories people share.

Leadership

Leaders play a pivotal role and should be held accountable for culture.

You will create a more comprehensive leadership development program separately, but you can use this meeting to gather suggestions, ideas, input, and perspective from the group about how they can interact more effectively with their leaders.

You can ask questions like:

- 'How can leaders help bridge the gap between the current and target culture?'

- 'What are the leadership behaviours needed to support the target culture?'

The feedback this group provides will be invaluable in helping you design the ideal leadership development program to create the target culture.

Systems

Systems are processes and procedures you have created in your business to improve efficiency and ensure consistent outcomes. Your group of people will need to consider how the systems of the organisation are impacting the culture and will impact the transition program. Systems can be created for things like:

- how people are promoted

- how people are performance managed

- how reviews are conducted

- how meetings are conducted

- procedures that must be followed.

Ask the group questions like:

- 'How are you spending most of your time?' This will help identify systems that are driving behaviour.

- 'Which systems are causing you the most headaches?' This will help identify systems that people have developed an 'attitudinal' response to.

- 'Which systems do you think we need to change to achieve our target culture?' This will help identify systems that will undermine or negate the target culture.

These conversations will give you plenty to discuss and address, and will help shape your culture plan.

Symbols

Symbolic gestures, activities, or items can have a dramatic effect on culture. The challenge for leaders is that something they do or a decision they make can have a symbolic significance without them realising.

People derive symbolic messages from things like:

- who gets promoted

- parking spaces

- where offices are located

- how often you visit them.

Your objective is to identify the symbolic items or activities which are having the biggest impact on the attitudes and behaviours in your organisation. You can then think about new activities or symbolic gestures that will highlight the transition from the current to the target culture.

Implement actions and Transform

This planning meeting will generate actions and give you everything you need to Transform your business. People are engaged, the process is simple, and there are well-defined actions with clear accountabilities.

You have created your own roadmap to greatness.

As you implement the actions you will transform your organisation from its current to the target culture.

The beauty of simplicity

The A.D.A.P.T. process can be summarised into one simple diagram (shown opposite) that illustrates the sound principles it's based on and the steps in the process. Implementing those steps will create a great culture.

INSPIRING GREATNESS

Chapter 10
How to lead a successful culture program

Culture is the attitudes and behaviours people adopt to fit in with the expectations of the people around them. The expectations that your people are most influenced by are communicated by the behaviour of your leaders. This means that your leaders need to role-model the right behaviours to create your target culture.

Most leaders find this a challenging idea because they are confused about how to behave to create the ideal culture. Most of the time culture is communicated and discussed through complicated data, graphs, charts, statistics, apps, and other hurdles.

How should you behave if you want to create a great culture? It's not something you can delegate to anyone else, particularly an external consultant. It's something you, as a leader, need to prioritise and action.

The best thing is keep it simple.

Define culture as the attitudes and behaviours people adopt to fit in, and involve yourself in conversations with your people about attitudes and behaviours.

You will achieve great results if you discuss the steps in A.D.A.P.T. Talk about your purpose, the attitudes and behaviours needed to deliver that purpose and how you can create those attitudes and behaviours.

It doesn't need to be any more complicated than that.

Facilitating A.D.A.P.T.

You will be more successful at implementing the A.D.A.P.T. process if you facilitate, which means you engage people in conversations where they contribute to the outcome.

A *great* facilitator engages a group because they want their contribution to make a decision and achieve an outcome. They invite divergent opinions and solve problems. They are more interested in the opinions of the group than their own. They operate from a belief that the wisdom of the group, if well facilitated, will deliver an outcome far superior to anything they could have come up with on their own. They do this because they passionately believe people commit to what they create.

An *average* facilitator knows the outcome that needs to be achieved but contributes their opinion and influences the group. They operate from a belief that they have all the answers and are the best person to solve the problems. As a result, people are less committed to the outcome because they don't feel they own the process.

A *shocking* facilitator knows the solution they want to implement before they begin and simply goes through the motions in the belief the group won't see through their charade. They shouldn't be called facilitators.

You don't need to learn specific skills to become a great facilitator. You need to see your role as being someone who helps *the group* achieve the outcome. Your purpose is to engage people in creating the solution so they are committed to the result. You need to believe the group contains the best people to create a new culture.

This can be hard for some leaders as they are much more comfortable with the idea they are the expert and have all the answers.

All you need to facilitate a great culture transformation is to be genuine, committed, humble, and willing to engage others in the process.

Being genuine

When you start asking people about culture you need to communicate, through your actions, that you are genuine. You can't be 'ticking a box' or 'paying lip service' to culture. It's not something that's on your 'to-do' list. It's too important for that.

People don't want to be disappointed, so they will watch your every move to make sure you are genuine and sincere. They are waiting to see if it *really is* a priority. They will assess this based on how you spend your time, effort, and money. If they see you putting more effort into something else, or prioritising other meetings, they will assume you are not genuine.

This is good news, because it means you don't need to be a brilliant facilitator, you just need to give it priority. They will help you with the rest. It doesn't matter if you make mistakes; *your people will help you.* You just need to put in the required time and effort. This will help people believe that you are genuine and they can be part of a great culture.

Being committed

You also need to be committed to a *great* culture.

A great culture is built on purpose and defined in a way that people can understand and consciously discuss. It will heavily involve your people, and create something they have always craved.

Don't settle for mediocrity. People want to be part of something *great.*

There will be cynics who refuse to believe it's possible, but if you keep listening and remain committed it *is* possible.

Being humble

This is, by far, the most important characteristic of a great leader.

If you are humble you can learn everything you need to know about building a great culture from your people. Just listen to them.

When it comes to culture, it's crazy to think that anyone has all the answers. There are no 'experts' on the culture of your organisation. Every culture is unique, so you will achieve more if you develop the skill of facilitating and listening to your people.

This doesn't mean you must do everything they say; it means you listen and balance their opinions with your own.

Humility is a willingness to listen and be influenced. It's an acknowledgement that everyone has a great contribution to make and you will achieve better outcomes if you listen.

Arrogance is a belief that you have all the answers and need to tell people what to do.

What type of leader would you prefer to work for?

Being willing to engage others

This is your secret to success. Engaging people in the process demonstrates that things will be different. You are willing to listen, understand the uniqueness of their culture, and acknowledge they *want* to be part of the process.

This helps people overcome their cynicism. When they see you behaving differently they will start to *believe* things will be different and they can achieve a great culture.

No-one believes it when you *say* 'it will be different this time'. They need to *see* a difference. Engaging them in the process demonstrates that you are genuine, committed, *and humble*.

The roadmap for the conversations

A.D.A.P.T. is the roadmap for the necessary conversations. Each step will engage your people in a way that will naturally and intuitively build a great culture.

You don't need to be an expert on culture; in fact, you may do better if you are *not* an expert. You don't need to be an experienced facilitator. You *do* need to engage your team, listen, and have the humility to learn.

The roadmap for the conversations

...

Chapter 11
How to develop successful leaders

Leaders play a vital role in creating the right culture. They are pivotal in *everything* you do. They deliver strategy, influence culture, and make decisions about every aspect of your business. One good decision by a leader could save or make millions of dollars. Conversely, a bad decision could cost millions.

But what does it cost when a leader has a bad effect on culture?

Most of the time you never know – but in 2015 German car manufacturer Volkswagen gave us a textbook example when it was discovered that they had deliberately cheated emissions tests using 'cheat software' that detected when the car was being driven under test conditions and adjusted emissions accordingly. What made this case extraordinary was the number of people that had to collaborate to make this possible.

Mr Larry Thompson, the US Justice Department–appointed monitor after the 'Dieselgate' scandal, stated 'there was a corrupt corporate culture at Volkswagen ... it was not a culture marked by honesty and openness'.

The scandal cost Volkswagen *billions*, and shattered their reputation globally.

It's an extreme example, but it raises the question, what does it cost if a leader impacts the culture in a negative way and causes a lot of people to make bad decisions?

On the flipside, what is the potential benefit if a leader impacts culture in a positive way and causes a lot of people to make good decisions? In 1992 Kotter and Heskett published a book called *Corporate Culture and Performance* in which they completed an extensive research project involving over 200 companies. They argued that a strong, constructive and adaptive culture produced strong financial results. One particular table highlighted differences in results over an 11-year period for 12 companies that had such a culture and 20 companies that did not. The results were startling.

Economic performance	Adaptive/ constructive culture	Non-adaptive/ defensive culture
Increase in revenue	682%	166%
Expansion of workforce	282%	36%
Growth of stock prices	901%	74%
Improvement of net incomes	756%	1%

Source: Kotter J.P. and Heskett J.L. (1992)

What is the potential benefit if a leader impacts culture in a positive way and causes a lot of people to make good decisions?

Developing strong leaders to have a positive effect on culture is an essential step in any cultural transformation. It's critical. The problem is that leadership development programs are having limited effect. Ask yourself, how much of any leadership development program is actually applied back at work?

Less than 10% of the concepts taught are applied; 90% of the effort and expense is wasted.

I heard these statistics so long ago I've lost track of where they came from, and yet in my experience they are true. How often have people in workshops talked about the challenges of applying what they are learning back at work? It has been like this for decades.

You will get more from your leadership development program if you follow these suggestions …

Provide context

It's surprising how often a company will implement a leadership development program without providing context or meaning for the participant.

People are more likely to apply what they have learned if they know and understand the context for the behaviours. Imagine teaching someone to kick a ball. How motivated would they be if you just taught them to kick a ball to another person and they kicked it back again? Would they become more motivated if they knew they were learning to play soccer, and they had a game coming up?

Context creates motivation. It gives meaning to what you are doing. When you create a target culture you are building a strong context for leadership development. It helps leaders focus on the specific attitudes and behaviours that will help build the target culture.

Work at a deeper level

Most leadership development programs are designed to teach skills or behaviour. If the statistics quoted on the previous page are even vaguely accurate this only works a small percentage of the time; the large majority of the skills are not applied back at work.

To create a meaningful change in leadership behaviour the program needs to be designed to create a transformation at a deeper level. The model below was developed by Robert Dilts, a well-known change therapist and organisational psychologist, and modified slightly to incorporate the 'iceberg' idea of deeper issues.

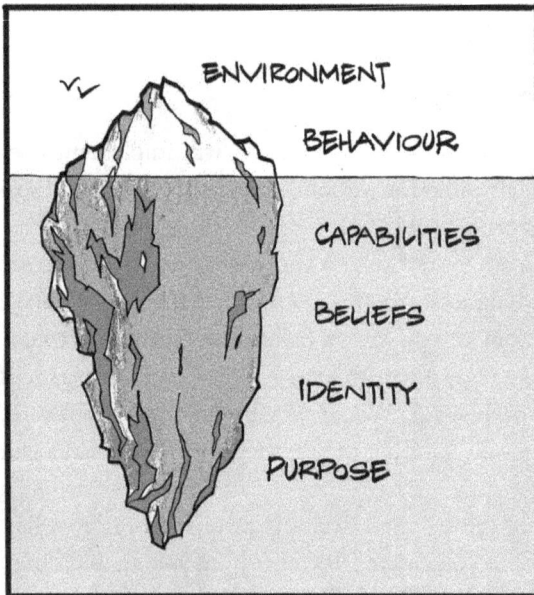

Dilts's theory is that transformational change occurs two levels 'deeper' than the issue.

This means that if someone wants to change behaviour, they need to change the *beliefs that drive the behaviour*. So, if you want your people to develop new skills or capabilities, you need to help them create a new identity.

It also means that if you work at the deepest level – being *purpose* – you will create a transformational change through all the levels. When someone develops a new understanding of their purpose they naturally and intuitively develop a new identity, beliefs, capabilities, and behaviour.

Very few leadership development programs are designed to create this type of transformation, but this is what's required if we want to create leaders who will intuitively build a great culture. Leaders first need to understand they exist to create a great culture, then they will see themselves differently, which will create new beliefs that will drive a new set of behaviours.

Explain role transitions

We need leaders to understand the transition they make as they move from one role to the next. People join a company with a specific expertise, and succeed through their *own effort*.

Their first promotion will usually be to a team leader role. But, they are chosen because they are the best at the *technical skill*.

In an effort to be successful, they will assign tasks, supervise the quality of work, give instruction, and solve problems. They will 'micro-manage'. At the time, in that role, that's appropriate and they will probably be successful.

The challenge is they are told this is 'leadership', and this creates beliefs about leadership like:

- a leader is the expert

- if you want something done correctly, do it yourself

- a leader needs to tell people what to do

- a leader gives instructions

- I can't assign them a task if I don't know how to do it myself.

- a leader takes on and solves problems for their team.

Their identity becomes linked to their ability to deliver the technical expertise, and they will see the purpose of their role, and leadership, as delivering outcomes by instructing, supervising, and micro-managing. Which is right; that *was* the purpose of their role *at that stage of their career.*

Their purpose 'iceberg' would look something like this:

Team leader
Behaviours: instruct, assign, micro-manage
Capabilities: technical skills
Beliefs: a leader instructs, assigns tasks, checks quality, and micro manages
Identity: I'm the person who delivers a technical outcome
Purpose: delivering technical outcomes by instructing, assigning, and micro-managing

But when they move to the next stage of their career the role will change. Instead of doing things themselves, they will need to delegate outcomes. Instead of assigning tasks they will need to clarify roles. Instead of micro-managing they will need to coach, mentor, and develop people.

In this role their purpose 'iceberg' would look something like this:

Manager
Behaviours: delegate, coach, clarify roles, develop people
Capabilities: people skills
Beliefs: a leader gives context, sets outcomes, and lets their people do the work
Identity: I am the person that clarifies expectations and targets
Purpose: to deliver outcomes by supporting and developing my people

The problem is that this behaviour will also be called 'leadership', despite the behaviours being very different.

Unless they make a successful transition from one role to the next, they will continue believing that leadership is micro-managing because that is the understanding they developed as a team leader and it's the meaning they now attach to that word. You can teach them new skills, but if that belief about the role doesn't change they will continue to micro-manage.

Do you have people in management positions who are still behaving like they are team leaders, or micro-managing? In a more senior role they need beliefs like:

- A leader clarifies roles (instead of doing all the work themselves).

- If you want something done correctly you need to coach and mentor people, otherwise you will end up doing it yourself.

- A leader needs to set clear goals, outcomes, and targets and let people decide what to do.

- A leader gives context, direction, and outcomes.

- A leader assigns outcomes, and may not always know how to do the task themselves.

- A leader engages their team to solve problems.

They will also need a new identity as a 'people leader', and will need to see the purpose of their role as setting their teams up for success instead of instructing, supervising, and micro-managing.

If they have a long and full career as a leader they will go through many transitions, so we need to get better at explaining the changes in what 'leadership' means as people progress through their careers. We need to stop using the word for such radically different behaviours and be specific about the purpose, identity, beliefs and subsequent behaviours needed for each role.

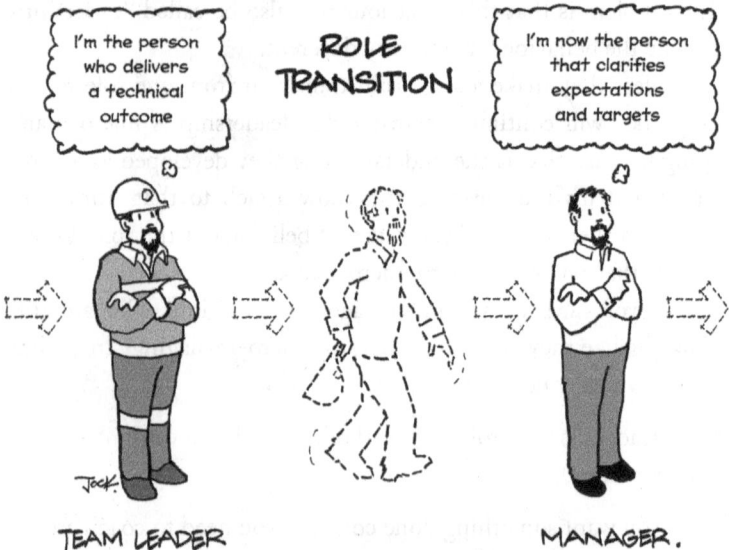

If your leadership development program doesn't highlight the significance of these transitions and build new beliefs, identity, and purpose, then behaviour won't change.

Involve their leader

Leadership workshops only contribute a small part of the return on investment from a leadership development program. Most of it will come from how the participants' direct supervisor, or leader, prepares them for the workshop and helps them integrate their learning back in the workplace.

A leader must talk to each participant about why they are attending the workshop, what they want them to learn, and how they will follow up and help them apply the concepts back in the workplace.

How often are your leaders having a conversation like that before one of their direct reports attends a leadership development workshop? It makes a huge difference, because the participant develops a clear understanding of why they are attending and realises their boss will expect them to apply what they have learned.

This can create a massive difference because it provides context for the workshop and concepts they will learn, and, if done well, will explain to the participant that they are moving to a new style of leadership.

What happens after a workshop is even more important.

If the leader provides coaching, support, and gives the participant the opportunity to implement their new skills, the return on investment dramatically improves.

Lead a culture program

When you initiate a culture program that aligns with purpose and defines a target culture, you are creating a strong context for leadership behaviours because it helps leaders understand the purpose of their role and create a new identity and beliefs. If you build a leadership development program that supports this level of transformation by explaining the transitions you will achieve great results.

Chapter 12
Engaging an external partner

Creating a great culture is often a partnership between you, your people, and an external provider.

It's almost impossible to be accurate about your own culture. The minute you become part of a culture you adopt the attitudes and behaviours of the group and no longer have an unbiased perspective. You may not even be aware this has happened. That's how culture works. How do you create a new culture if you can't see some of the unique characteristics of your current culture?

Another question is whether someone who works full time for an organisation, and therefore relies on the company and its leadership for their survival, can provide objective feedback about the culture, particularly if there are problems.

So, you will need an external perspective from someone who is not dependent on your company for their survival.

Who does what?

You and your people will need to do most of the work, mainly because you are the only ones that can create a new culture, but there is a role for an external partner. Their perspective will be vital in helping you understand the attitudes and behaviours in your business.

Your role

This includes:

- engaging in conversations with your teams about culture and making it conscious

- facilitating, or participating in, the conversation to align culture with purpose and define a target culture

- facilitating, or participating in, the planning

- delivering on action items that were delegated to you during the planning.

You will also need to be very aware of how your behaviour is being interpreted. Your team will learn from what you do, not just what you say. You will need to invite feedback and pay attention to how people react to your suggestions and decisions.

You will need to spend time coaching and supporting your leaders as they cascade the conversations throughout the organisation and engage with their teams. They will need support as they begin to understand the changes in their role and develop the purpose, identity and beliefs necessary to guide their teams through the A.D.A.P.T. process.

There will be a lot of coaching, reviewing, and learning as you engage in the program, but you will find this easy if you are genuine, committed, humble and engage your people in the process.

Your external partner's role

Getting this role right is a balancing act between refusing to engage an external perspective and letting them do too much.

Your external partner needs to be someone who sees their role as supporting you through the process. They will need to value your opinion more than their own and embrace the decisions you make about your culture.

You need to make the decisions because it's *your* business, purpose and culture.

Avoid people who present themselves as the expert on your culture and who tell you what your culture should be, or who use an instrument that dictates a predetermined target culture. They are violating the principles we looked at earlier and will make the process hard work.

The primary function of your external partner is to support you to engage your people in the decisions that will define your purpose and culture.

They are a partner, not an implementer. A coach, not a consultant.

They will coach and guide you in the steps. They can give you advice, support, even instruction, but you and your team need to make the decisions. Think of it this way: your partner can tell you the questions you need to answer but must let you and your team answer them.

Your external partner should do the following:

- provide a structure for you to follow, ideally something like the A.D.A.P.T. process that follows sound principles

- coach you in the conversations you need to have with your team, and give you guidance, support, and feedback that will help you improve those conversations

- assess and provide an external and unbiased perspective on your current culture

- facilitate conversations that will help you make decisions and transform your business.

Choosing a Good External Partner

I'VE GOT THE RIGHT QUALIFICATIONS FOR YOU

I'VE GOT THE RIGHT INDUSTRY EXPERIENCE FOR YOU

I'VE GOT THE RIGHT VALUE PROPOSITION FOR YOU

I'VE GOT THE RIGHT PROCESS FOR YOU

I'VE GOT THE RIGHT CULTURAL SENSITIVITIES

YOU'LL KNOW IT
WHEN YOU SEE IT

Finding the right facilitation style

Whoever facilitates the conversations, whether it's you or your external partner, it's critical they let the group make their own decisions.

In simple terms the role of the facilitator is to:

- make sure the objective of any discussion is clear and understood by all

- make sure the group has strong ground rules for the discussion

- clarify the group decision-making process. Will the leader make the final decision? Will a decision only be made if the group is unanimous? How much of a majority is required to carry a decision if you are voting?

- keep the discussion focused on the objective

- invite divergent opinions and make sure everyone is heard

- control outspoken people if they think they are acting in a way that will stifle the conversation or contributions from others

- apply a problem-solving or planning process if needed

- support the group to make a decision.

They need to do all this *without influencing the outcome*.

The benefits of using an external facilitator

I am often asked about the benefits of using an external facilitator. A simple way to answer this is to look at the facilitation style that is required. Could you perform those functions without influencing the outcome? If the answer is no then you will benefit from using an external facilitator.

Choose wisely. Facilitators who support a group to make decisions, *without influencing the outcome*, are rare.

A.D.A.P.T. roles and an external facilitator

The only step in the A.D.A.P.T. process that *requires* an external perspective is **A**ssessing current culture. It's critical that an independent and unbiased assessor conducts the interviews and focus groups.

There are many reasons for this:

- People will open up more to an external assessor.

- It protects confidentiality.

- An external assessor will interpret *all* the messages, including unspoken messages, through an unbiased perspective.

- They can also compare the attitudes and behaviours in the business with other companies they have assessed.

- People find it easier to accept feedback from an 'external' perspective.

Engaging an external partner to facilitate the other steps in the A.D.A.P.T. process is optional. You will benefit from an external perspective but it's not *essential*.

The essential part is that you *have* the conversations.

Chapter 13
Measuring the results

One of the most consistent questions I am asked is, 'how will we measure the results?'

To answer this, ask yourself: how are you measuring results *now*?

If it ain't broke

Most people initiate a culture program because of a reactive response to a frustrating situation. They might be frustrated by the behaviour in their team or organisation, or finding it hard to get things done, or alarmed at the results the company is achieving. They might be losing people, or experiencing a lot of sick leave, and wondering if it's a cultural problem.

The point is that most people are happy to initiate a culture program in response to an anecdotal or *subjective* observation. They are frustrated or concerned with the current situation, or excited about the prospect of a new culture, and that feeling drives them to initiate a culture program.

So why would you try to impose a different style of assessment in the future?

If the anecdotal and subjective assessment was strong enough to initiate the investment in a culture program, what's wrong with using it to continue the assessment? It's simple, natural, and logical to embrace the measures you already have in place, whatever they are, and continue using them as you move forward.

If you are alarmed that people are leaving then make staff retention one of your 'measures'.

If you are frustrated you can't get anything done then start measuring how effectively you deliver projects, or implement new ideas.

If you are frustrated by the behaviour in your team then take note of that behaviour and check your frustration levels in the future.

The desire to create some new sort of artificial measure is one of the biggest problems in 'culture change'. It just adds complexity and creates confusion. It's far more effective to be conscious of the measures you are currently using and use them in the future.

Recording and monitoring progress

It's a simple process to record a subjective feeling about an issue so you can measure against it in the future. One of the reasons interviews and focus groups are so powerful is they do this for you. You just need to capture and record the 'feeling' in whatever form it is expressed. You can then do the same thing a year or two later and compare the results.

It's simple, effective, and can lead to wonderful conversations. For example: 'two years ago you were frustrated, now you are excited – what has changed?', or, 'a year ago there was a significant lack of trust that stopped people embracing ideas, now you are talking to each other and making suggestions – why?'.

What type of conversation would you prefer to participate in? 'We've had an 8% improvement in our culture', or, 'we are embracing new ideas and making our own suggestions'?

The right conversation can become a lot of fun. Often people will start making fun of themselves and how they used to behave: 'I can't believe we used to do that!'

Everything is subjective

It's time to accept the subjectivity inherent in all cultural assessments.

If you use a survey you will experience subjectivity. People are influenced by how they feel when they answer the questions, and there will be significant 'interpretation' when you discuss the results. Even the survey itself will have built-in subjective elements. And have you noticed that statistics are always open to interpretation?

Culture is a naturally evolving and subjective experience. If you try to quantify it you will make it difficult to understand, which leads to complicated discussions that are often about statistics and everything *but* the culture.

Keep it simple. Talk about the attitudes and behaviours and accept the fact that you will get different interpretations and perceptions. That's a good thing because it will lead to a richer conversation and a deeper understanding of the organisational culture.

Remember, the conversation is the most important part of this process.

The strength of interviews and focus groups

This is another reason to use interviews and focus groups to assess your culture. You can tailor the questions based on the subjective assessment that initiated your culture program.

One client of mine initiated a culture program out of frustration with their staff. They had a highly unionised workforce that resisted every suggestion to improve their manufacturing process. It was frustrating because some of the suggestions would make life easier but the workers resisted them anyway.

As we conducted a culture assessment we included questions designed to help us understand the attitudes and behaviours that were driving this issue. We identified a deep lack of trust because of poor relationships. The workers resisted because they constantly felt like managers were 'out to get them'.

We accepted this as an aspect of the current culture, and when we did another assessment two years later we included similar questions to assess these specific attitudes and behaviours.

The most significant improvement identified was the workers were now *making* suggestions for process improvement.
It was great feedback that we were successfully creating a new culture.

The ultimate measure

The ultimate measure of any culture program is business performance. What improvements are you noticing? In the example above they achieved a 9% increase in productivity with slightly lower costs, which yielded a massive 50% increase in profit.

What business measures are you hoping to improve? A reduction in absenteeism? An improvement in retention? Productivity improvements? Delivery of projects? Cost reduction?

Anything is possible if you align with purpose and define your target culture.

Chapter 14
Other applications of A.D.A.P.T.

The A.D.A.P.T. process is simple and flexible enough that it can be used by any group which has a culture. Let's have a look …

Sports teams

If you are the captain or coach of a sporting team, a conversation about why you play the game (**A**lign with purpose) and the culture you need (**D**efine target culture) can lead to a different level of inspiration and motivation.

> For example, one team I worked with decided they played to 'inspire' fans. They were from a sport that struggled to get participation and attendance at games. They realised that great achievements on the sporting field can inspire and motivate people in powerful ways, and at the very least it might inspire people to participate in the sport and attend games.
>
> It became a powerful motivation for what they were doing. They were 'playing to inspire'.

They decided they needed a culture of 'support'. They chose to support each other no matter what. They came to this decision because they knew that trying to do something 'inspirational' might be a risk. It takes courage to attempt an inspirational act, so they decided to support each other no matter the outcome. If the risk didn't pay off the individual was still supported.

Imagine that. How would the performance of your team change if they were playing to 'inspire' and knew they had 'support' no matter what?

Assessing their culture wasn't difficult; they were a small team. Planning the steps needed to implement a Transformation was even easier. They did it together as a group. When they aligned to a common purpose and decided to support each other the rest was easy.

Other groups

Any group will benefit from the conversations in the A.D.A.P.T. process:

- educational institutions

- religious groups

- the military

- not-for-profit organisations or charities

- government departments

- corrections organisations

- small, medium, or large companies.

The only thing that changes is how you apply the A.D.A.P.T. conversations.

In a small company or group, you can engage the whole organisation.

In larger companies your leaders will need to cascade the conversations throughout the organisation. As we've seen, you may end up with slightly different expressions of purpose and culture, but that won't matter because they will all be aligned to a consistent theme. In fact, it's an advantage because it means people have thought about the purpose of the organisation and the culture needed to deliver that purpose, and how they fit into this.

That is the power of the A.D.A.P.T. process. Your entire organisation will be aligned to a common purpose and working towards creating the ideal culture to deliver that purpose.

Hands up all the people who want to work in *that* company?

Conclusion

Culture is the attitudes and behaviours people adopt to fit in with the expectations of the people around them, which are communicated through the stories, leadership, systems, and symbols of the organisation.

If you want to create a great culture the first, and easiest, step is to start talking about culture and make it the attitudes and behaviours people *consciously* adopt.

When you start having these conversations you will be amazed at the response. People want to be part of a great culture, and they will contribute to the process if they believe you are genuine, committed, humble, and willing to engage them in the process.

ENGAGING CULTURE

A.D.A.P.T. is a roadmap for the conversations that will lead to a *great* culture. It follows the principles described in chapter 2 – which influence your organisation whether you like it or not – and makes your culture program easier. It succeeds because it's simple and engaging and can be implemented by leaders at every level of the organisation.

As you engage people in these discussions you will build a sense of security, safety, belonging, and purpose that will help your people achieve their full potential.

To create a new culture you need to:

- **A**lign with purpose – answer the question 'why do we exist?'.

- **D**efine target culture – in one word, or two at the most, so that everyone can talk about it.

- **A**ssess current culture – by using an external partner to run interviews and focus groups.

- **P**lan – by engaging a representative sample of people from the company.

- **T**ransform – by reframing stories and developing leaders, systems, and symbols that support your target culture.

When you do this you are creating attitudes and behaviours that people will consciously discuss, adopt, and expect from each other to deliver the purpose and strategy of the organisation.

Achieving greatness

Engaging with people to work together and create a culture that will deliver the purpose of the organisation is one of the most uplifting and fantastic things you will ever do. There is a sense of commitment, pride, and passion that is hard to describe. Think about how much people (perhaps secretly) want to be part of a great culture, and then imagine how they will feel when they achieve it. Lives will change for the better as people learn to communicate and work together towards a common purpose.

It's easier than you think. You can make mistakes so long as you remain genuine, committed and humble. Your people will help you because they desperately want you to be successful at this particular endeavour.

Taking your first step

If you are not sure what to do next, try starting a conversation with one of your colleagues or trusted and helpful employees. Ask them something like, 'What do you think of the culture here?'

As they answer, think about what they have said. Did they show any awareness of a purpose and desired culture for the business? Are they just talking about whether or not people get along, or are they demonstrating a deeper understanding of culture?

You will quickly realise that people want to engage in this conversation, and hopefully that will inspire you to start conversations about the purpose of the company and the culture needed to deliver that purpose.

From that point, great things can happen.

The beauty of the A.D.A.P.T. model is that it can be as structured or unstructured as you like. You can follow the process in general conversations, or you can structure a culture program that will create a great culture capable of achieving amazing results.

If you are thinking about a culture program, I encourage you to do three things:

1. Write down all the reasons you would like to create a new culture for your business – the things that are frustrating you and the things you would like to achieve. They will form the basis of your measures.

2. Write down the attitudes and behaviours that you believe currently exist and are forming the current culture of your organisation. What attitudes and behaviours do people need to adopt to 'fit in'?

3. Start talking to your people about the culture in the business, why the company exists, and the culture they think is needed to achieve amazing results.

When you have done that you will be motivated to go back to chapter 6 and think about how to initiate the conversations to Align with Purpose, and that will start you on an amazing transformation.

Your people are your culture, so start talking to them, listen to them, and together you can achieve greatness.

Some of the most satisfying experiences I have ever had have been walking back into a workplace where we have achieved a significant cultural transformation. People are happier, friendlier, more positive, supportive, and welcoming, and they are achieving better results through less effort because communication, cooperation, teamwork, and interpersonal relationships have significantly improved.

And *that's* something to look forward to.

Index